GETTING A GRIP ON TIME MANAGEMENT

Finding Time for Effective Youth Ministry

Les Christie

VICTOR
BOOKS a division of SP Publications, Inc.

WHEATON, ILLINOIS 60187

Offices also in
Whitby, Ontario, Canada
Amersham-on-the-Hill, Bucks, England

The author is most grateful to the following film
libraries for assistance in obtaining the photographs
contained in this book:
    Eddie Brandt's Saturday Matinee, Hollywood
    Larry Edmunds Bookstore, Hollywood
    Movie Star News, New York City

Cover photo used with permission of the Harold Lloyd Estates
from the film "Safety Last," 1923.

Edwin Arlington Robinson, "Richard Cory" from The Children
of the Night. Copyright under the Berne Convention. Re-
printed with the permission of Charles Scribner's Sons.

Quotations from the "Twilight Zone" episode, "Walking
Distance," are from The Twilight Zone Companion, Marc Scott
Zicree, © 1982 by Marc Scott Zicree. By permission of
Bantam Books, Inc. All rights reserved.

All Bible quotations, unless otherwise noted, are from the
Holy Bible: New International Version, © 1978 by the New
York International Bible Society. Other quotations are from
the New American Standard Bible (NASB), © the Lockman Founda-
tion 1960, 1962, 1963, 1968, 1971, 1972, 1973, 1975, 1977,
and the King James Version (KJV).

Library of Congress Catalog Card Number: 83-51746
ISBN: 0-88207-192-0

VICTOR BOOKS
A division of SP Publications, Inc.
Wheaton, Ill. 60187

CONTENTS

PREFACE

<u>Getting a Grip On Time Management</u> is for the veteran, the rookie, the volunteer, and the professional. My hope is that its contents will assist you in investing your time creatively so you can avoid burnout and handle stress positively. This book is not a cure-all with six easy steps, but it <u>will</u> point you in the right direction by giving you some practical handles to start managing your life.

I am dedicating this book to: Jim Irby III, George and Naomi Curry, Tim Coop, Dick Miller, Ben Merold, Wayne Rice, Mike Yaconelli, and Tic Long.

"Hold fast the time. Guard it, watch over it, every hour, every minute, un-
guarded it slips away, like a lizard, smooth, slippery, faithless. Hold every
minute sacred."

Thomas Mann

WHITE RABBITS, PLATE SPINNERS, AND YOUTH WORKERS

CHAPTER ONE

The first time I read Lewis Carroll's literary classic <u>Alice in Wonderland</u> my attention was drawn to the White Rabbit. Though he is mentioned several times in the book, his character is never really developed. I wanted to get to know him better, but he was always in such a hurry.

Whenever Alice would get close to the White Rabbit he would pull out his watch from his waistcoat pocket and quickly pop down a hole under a hedge or scurry down some long passage. It was almost as if he didn't want to get to know Alice--to reveal his true self to her or anyone else. Whenever he <u>did</u> say anything it was usually limited to, "Oh dear, Oh dear, I shall be too late," or, "Oh my ears and whiskers, how late it's getting!" He always struck me as out-of-breath, flustered, and inaccessible.

I think I was attracted to the White Rabbit because I saw so much of him reflected in my own style of youth ministry. I would run around at a frantic pace, ignoring the very people I was called to minister to because I had "more important things to do"--things like picking up a Christian film, setting up chairs for an activity, going to a committee meeting, or designing publicity for a special event.

I was keeping busy, but I was losing perspective on my ministry. The genuinely important items were being put on the back burner. Auren Uris wrote, "Many in the high pressure world . . . look on helplessly while their responsibilities grow faster than they can handle them" (Ted Engstrom and R. Alex Mackenzie, <u>Managing Your Time</u>, Zondervan, p. 175). That was me!

My ministry was beginning to resemble a circus performer's plate-spinning act. He starts by spinning a few plates on a couple of long, thin wooden poles. Quickly he adds more poles and plates as he runs back and forth to keep the original ones going. This artist is always on the move, trying to keep all the plates spinning simultaneously.

The world record for plate spinning is held by Shukuni Sasaki of Japan. On July 16, 1981 he had 72 plates spinning at the same time. I think there were times in my ministry when I put Shukuni to shame with the number of programs I had spinning. When I wasn't adding more plates to the poles, someone else was adding them for me.

Most youth workers I know are busy, hard-working men and women. They are in youth ministry because they have a deep love for young people and a desire to reach them for Christ. The tragedy is that after a few months of ministry, many of them begin to resemble the White Rabbit, or a plate spinner.

Usually a youth worker starts out with great intentions. But sooner or later he gets so bogged down in meetings and programs that he no longer has time for the young people who are the object of his ministry.

He runs around at a frantic pace, but accomplishes little for the Lord or His kingdom. Eventually he becomes even more disorganized till finally he loses all perspective on his ministry.

We Are Examples

As youth workers we are called to be examples to our young people. Paul tells Timothy, "Set an example" (1 Timothy 4:12). That includes being examples in how we manage our time. The Bible makes us aware that, "A student is not above his teacher, but everyone who is fully trained will be like his teacher" (Luke 6:40).

I have gone to the same stationery store for the last 13 years. One day last year I rushed into the store to make a purchase, and two new salespeople wrote up my order. In my hurry, I scribbled my last name on the charge slip, inadvertently omitting the last two letters of "Christie." As I left, I overheard one salesperson ask the

I THINK I HEAR ANOTHER YOUTH WORKER ABOUT TO BURN OUT.

other, "Who was that guy?" The other glanced down at the charge slip, saw the name "Christ," and with a surprised look replied, "Oh my, it's the boss Himself."

Something I had been telling my youth for years hit me square in the face that day. As Christians, we are reflectors of Christ in this world. We are to mirror the image of Christ.

What kind of time management examples do we set for young people in our groups and communities? Are we always in a hurry? Do we appear too busy for people?

The earthly ministry of Jesus Christ points out some helpful principles about the general use of time. Though Christ knew His time on earth was limited, He never showed signs of being hurried or pressured. He became physically tired on occasion, but He never appeared emotionally frustrated due to lack of time. Yet many frustrated people in youth ministry today seem to be constantly playing "catch-up ball."

The purpose of this book is not to make you feel guilty or give you extra "work" to do. The goal of this book is to help you organize your life so that you will have more time to do those things that are important to you and to the Lord.

Some of you may be burned out, on the verge of throwing in the towel or turning in your youth worker's badge. At this point in your ministry you may feel swamped, weary, stale, fatigued, or totally exhausted. You may be overcommitted, over-exerted, overtired, overloaded, overworked, overdriven, and over a barrel. Physically you may look tired, worn, faint, bored, and haggard.

I can sympathize with you. I remember vividly the many times I would drag myself into my home late at night after a long day of youth ministry and begin to question what I had <u>really</u> accomplished. How many lives had been changed? Had I used my time wisely?

I am hoping this book will get you back on your feet with some practical, helpful handles before you bid farewell to youth ministry and become a trainee at K-Mart or McDonald's. You can learn to manage your time better. And that, in turn, will make you a more effective youth worker.

Burnout in Youth Ministry

Youth ministry is a prime target for burnout because of an imbalance: Youth workers are supposed to be giving, supportive, good listeners, empathetic, and open to relationships. This posture demands huge investments of time, emotional energy, and responsibility with little feedback and often little or no recognition. Imbalance seems to be inevitable, and it certainly is draining!

Youth workers, who are in intimate contact with people's pains and problems, often extend themselves beyond reasonable limits. Youth workers tend to have high expectations of themselves. These must be juxtaposed with the expectations of others in their ministry (parents, board members, other adult workers, and the young people themselves). Burnout begins when a youth worker fails to produce the expected results.

A youth worker on the verge of burnout may have the following visible signs:

- Many incompleted tasks
- Jobs stacking up
- Disordered relationships
- Lack of quality conversation with a spouse, roommate, or good friend
- A cluttered, disorganized desk
- Forgotten appointments
- Missed deadlines
- Broken promises
- Time invested in increasingly unproductive tasks
- Unsatisfactory spiritual life
- Blaming others (parents, minister, board, youth)
- A tendency to work harder, while accomplishing less and less

9

A sense of flailing away in every direction at the work that needs to be done

Pretending not to understand what is happening

Michael Mitchell, author of <u>Consultant Burn-Out</u> (University Associate, Inc.), describes three stages of burnout: physical, psychological, and spiritual. <u>Physical fatigue</u> includes feelings of being continually tired and lethargic. Colds, flu, aches, and pains are common at this stage. Whether the fatigue is real or not, the feelings are there. It's as if the youth worker's body takes responsibility for temporarily withdrawing him from the action.

The second stage is <u>psychological fatigue</u>. This stage includes many of the physical symptoms. A burned-out youth worker feels alienated from his work and his young people. He feels emotionally exhausted. He gets up in the morning and still feels tired after eight hours of sleep. He becomes impatient with people, drums his fingers on his desk, and sighs deeply after receiving even the smallest request or task. He tends to become callous toward people and to start treating them like objects or numbers. He may show an increased desire for variety and uniqueness in youth ministry activities. He has difficulty investing himself in the youth. He reasons, "I need to conserve energy because everyone wants a piece of me and there isn't enough to go around."

Feeling alone, alienated, tired, and bored, the burned-out youth worker easily moves to the third stage, <u>spiritual fatigue</u>. He thinks about changing jobs. He begins to give up aspirations, dreams, hope, zeal, and yearns to "hide out" for a while, becoming a loner. He starts to agree with the bumper sticker: "The more I know people, the more I like my dog." He considers moving to a different area, or even moving to an entirely new profession. He doubts his effectiveness and begins to wonder, "Who am I doing this for, anyway? Do I really make any difference in the kids' lives?" At this point, a youth worker's ability to invest in teens drops even lower.

The stages of burnout--physical, psychological, and spiritual--culminate in overall burnout when a person hits the bottom of the well. Anyone can be a victim. The Bible records how Elijah suffered from burnout, even though he was obedient to the Lord and had a successful ministry. He single-handedly took on 450 prophets of Baal (1 Kings 18:17-46). Yet when Queen Jezebel said, "I'm going to kill you," he ran 120 miles in the opposite direction! (1 Kings 19:1-3)

Burnout is a depletion of emotional resources. Elijah was so exhausted, he laid under a bush and prayed to the Lord that he might die.

Youth workers, Elijah didn't want to die! If he <u>really</u> wanted to die, I know a woman 120 miles back up the road who would have been glad to accommodate him. Have you ever thanked God for unanswered prayer? I think Elijah did on that day. He was simply exhausted.

When You Can't Hold On Any Longer

At a recent conference, Gordon MacDonald told a story of one of the most dramatic events in the circus world. Several years ago at Detroit's Cobo Hall with Ringling Brothers, Barnum and Bailey Circus, the climactic event of the night was the high-wire act of the flying Wallenda family. They were probably the greatest tightwire walkers of all circus history.

One of the acts was the formation of a four-level pyramid on the tightrope. Four or five men made the first level, two or three were added for the second, two more on the third, and finally a little girl climbed to the very top. In this four-level pyramid, they would make their way from one side of the wire to the other. It was incredible and unprecedented. And they had been doing it night after night, month after month, around the world.

This particular evening, as the show came to its conclusion, the four-level pyramid act was about to begin. The arena was dark. The audience was in total silence. Spotlights shone on the performers in the air as they started moving across the wire. About two thirds of the way across the wire one of the men on the first level cried out in German, "I cannot hold on any longer!" and the entire pyramid collapsed. Several of the Wallendas fell to the floor below. Some were crippled for life and one died.

This story reminds me of what we are seeing with tragic regularity in youth ministry. Men and women who serve Jesus Christ with vigor, vitality, force, and excitement seem incredibly successful. Then one day we hear, "I cannot hold on any longer!" Unfortunately, we are often too late in picking up the signals of those around us.

I remember reading the poem "Richard Cory" by Edwin Arlington Robinson in high school.

Richard Cory

Whenever Richard Cory went downtown,
We people on the pavement looked at him.
He was a gentleman from sole to crown.
Clean favored and imperially slim,
And he always was quietly arrayed
And he was always human when he talked;
But still he fluttered pulses when he said,
"Good morning" and he glittered when he walked,
And he was rich--yes, richer than a king.
And admirably schooled in every grace:
In time, we thought he was everything
To make us wish that we were in his place.
So on we worked, and waited for the light,
And went without the meat, and cursed the bread;
And Richard Cory, one calm summer night,
Went home and put a bullet through his head.

(The Children of the Night,
Charles Scribner's Sons)

I was told in college that a renowned
British evangelist once said, "It is better
to burn out than to rust out." That
statement is just not true! Don't misunder-
stand me; I am not saying God honors
laziness. But once you have burned
out, there is nothing left to give.

Hot Line to Help

Alcoholics Anonymous and Weight Watchers
have one thing in common. They each have a
24-hour hot line that you can call from
anywhere in the United States. When you
call the number you reach someone with an
understanding heart and a listening ear,
who has felt the same urges you now feel.

Wouldn't it be wonderful if youth
workers could have an 800 number to another sympathetic youth worker? Prayer
is an 800 number to a sympathetic God who
cares and understands. He is the real
source of strength. Too many times we
worry about future events instead of
trusting God to do things His way.

The essential root of burnout is a
spiritual problem. We burn out because

YOUTH WORKER HOT LINE. WHAT'S YOUR PROBLEM, DEARIE?

we try to do our jobs in our own strength rather than in the grace of God. Instead of becoming spiritual warriors, we become emotional wrecks.

Prayer has been a real source of encouragement to me when I have been on the verge of calling it quits. I keep a prayertime diary in which I record specific prayer requests and the date. In a parallel column I list God's answers and the date they come.

When I feel "down," I flip through my prayertime diary and reflect on how God has answered my requests in the past. God's time schedule and unique way are hard to understand sometimes. I receive added confidence by looking with hindsight and realizing how God is in control.

Ask yourself this question: "Is God nervous about the upcoming retreat, youth drama, or board meeting? Is He biting His nails?" Then why are you? Whose ministry is this? At what pace does God operate?

Another help to me has been to keep letters, postcards, and notes kids have written me over the years. I can thumb through these when I get that sinking feeling and remember that I have some value.

Photographs have also been helpful during my rocky times. Looking back and remembering great times with my youth group always seems to boost my spirits. Prayer and reminiscing are two effective ways to handle the pressure of youth ministry.

Standing Up Under Stress

Stress can be beneficial and guide us to a better relationship with Christ, or it can lead to burnout.

Stress is actually an engineering term for the amount of pressure something can take before it snaps. For example, engineers know the exact amount of pressure

the cables on the Golden Gate Bridge can
take before they snap. Do you know the
amount of pressure <u>you</u> can take (before you
break)?

Stress can be a motivator if we react to
it in the correct way. It can help us meet
deadlines and turn in reports. It can keep
our jobs from becoming monotonous. But the
key is how we <u>respond</u> when stress jumps out
at us.

In youth work it is easy to become
overwhelmed by responsibilities. Each of
us has agonized over tasks that must
be done, projects that must be planned, or
people we must see. But time can slip away
from a caring, involved youth worker,
unnoticed and unaccounted for.

Have you ever asked, "Where does that
youth worker get the time to do those
things?" The truth is that no one has
more time than you do--and no one has less.
Each of us has 60 minutes in an hour, 168
hours in a week, and 52 weeks in a year.
The other guy's watches and clocks run at
the same rate as yours.

It has been said that time is like money
and must be wisely spent. But unlike
money, we <u>have</u> to spend time. You cannot
"save" it. You can only use it. It cannot
be hoarded, banked, or borrowed. The
question each of us must ponder is, "How
wisely are we spending our time?"

We may "stop the clock" on a basketball
court or football field, but never in the
game of life. Yesterday is a canceled
check. Tomorrow is simply a promissory
note.

Have you ever asked, "Where did the time
go?" As Albert Einstein explained, "Time
is relative." Practically, we can begin to
understand his theory when time seems
to pass faster or slower. For example,
time drags when our football team is
winning by only two points with three
minutes left on the clock. But time flies
when our football team is losing by only
two points with three minutes on the
clock.

One hour on a baseball field is different from one hour in a classroom. Time is slower for the student than for the teacher. It is slower for the congregation than it is for the preacher. As the saying goes, "Time flies when you're having fun." But time seems to drag when you're not.

Time can be cruel. You're familiar with "bad timing," like when:

☐ You take cover from a sudden downpour in the doorway of a porno movie house and the chairman of your board passes by.
☐ The restaurant in which you just finished eating a huge meal is raided by the Health Department . . . and condemned.
☐ Diarrhea hits while you're stuck in rush-hour traffic.
☐ You plan a ski trip the same day your hometown football team makes it to the state finals for the first time in 25 years.
☐ Your nose starts to run and you don't have a handkerchief.

The Bible has much to say about time and how we use it. Look up the verses below and pray about how your time is being used. Are you in control, or does your schedule control you?

Time is limited.	Job 14:14
Word of Lord abides forever	Acts 17:26
	1 Peter 1:24-25
Time is adequate.	2 Timothy 4:5
fulfill your ministry	
Time is important.	1 Corinthians 9:24
Run w/it	Hebrews 12:1
Time can be misused.	Ecclesiastes 7:17
Time should be controlled.	Galatians 5:22-23

We need to pray the prayer of Moses: "Teach us to number our days aright, that we may gain a heart of wisdom" (Psalm 90:12). Paul urges us over and over again to manage our time well. He exhorts us, "Make the most of every opportunity" to manage our time well. He exhorts us, "Make the most of every opportunity" (Colossians 4:5). The biblical term "redeeming the time" (Colossians 4:5 and Ephesians 5:16, KJV) does not refer just to minutes and hours. It also means having an awareness of the opportunities that arise to extend the kingdom to others. These Bible verses deal with discerning priorities.

Don't Let Others Set the Pace for You

During my seminary years I can remember reading biographies of great men and women who boldly reached their world for Jesus Christ. I would sit in awe as I read of those who got up at 4 a.m. to pray for an hour before beginning their day at 5 a.m. I was so convicted that I tried to become like all the people I had studied under and read about. Instead, I became more like the beast in the Book of Daniel. I was part gold, part silver, part brass, and had clay feet. At first I felt guilty. Then it dawned on me that God did not expect me to be exactly like someone else.

God made each of us unique. You may be a morning person or a night person. You may only need four hours sleep, or you may need a full nine hours. You may be the kind of person who gets drowsy or hits a slump in the late afternoon.

Try to figure out your internal "prime time"--the time you are at your best--and capitalize on it. When are you in high gear? Fairly alert? In low gear? Out of it?

Use the suggestions in this book as guidelines only. Apply them, but make sure you consider your organizational structure and your own body cycle. Set your own pace, and learn to let time work for (instead of against) you.

I FELL ASLEEP DURING MORNING PRAYER TIME. WHAT ARE YOU IN FOR?

Time Wasters and Robbers

Be warned that there are nasty critters in this world that will try to waste or rob your time. Be on the alert for:

Interruptions	Family errands
Procrastination	Failure to delegate
Indecision	Lack of preparation
Misplaced items	Telephone interruptions
Junk mail	Detail work
Drop-in visitors	Meetings
Waiting for people	Destructive attitudes
Television	Reading unnecessary material
Lack of goals	Mediocre staff
Family problems	Poor organization
Commuting time	

Taken from Tools for Time Management (Edward R. Dayton, Zondervan. Used by permission.)

Time to Respond

1. Which of the following characters do you identify with in the area of time management?

    ___ White Rabbit   ___ Road Runner
    ___ Charlie Brown   ___ Speedy Gonzales
    _X_ Superman   ___ Rip Van Winkle

    Why? *always come up in the last minute*

2. Are you in one of the three stages of burnout?

    Which one: ___ Physical
                    ___ Psychological
                    ___ Spiritual

    What are your symptoms?

3. What activity do you enjoy most in your ministry? *Counseling*

    How much time do you spend doing that? *1 hr/wk*

    What activity do you enjoy least in youth ministry? *planning little details*

    How much time do you spend doing that? *30 hrs/wk*

4. What time of the day are you in high gear? Fairly alert? In low gear? Out of it?

    high - am
    fair - afternoon
    low -

5. What critters are wasting and robbing your time? *waiting, lack of goals*
    detail wk, failure to delegat

6. What do these verses teach about our use of time?

    Psalm 90:12 *wise use of t overcomes evil*
    Ephesians 5:16
    Colossians 4:5 *time is redeemed, it glorifies God*
    1 Timothy 4:12 *can be an example for others*

GOALS AND PRIORITIES

CHAPTER TWO

Goal-oriented youth workers <u>know</u> where they are headed with their own lives and with the lives of the young people God has entrusted to them. Goal-oriented youth workers are dreamers who envision what God can do in and through their young people and staff members.

Clearly-defined goals put handles on your dreams. I remember John F. Kennedy's pronouncement in 1960 that the U.S. would put a man on the moon in 10 years. That vision seemed unrealistic and unattainable. But goals were established, target dates were set, and the dream was kept in the forefront of people's thoughts. Then on July 20, 1969, Neil Armstrong stepped onto the moon.

Goal-oriented people take criticism and handle rejection better than those who have no goals. It is better to have a goal and not reach it, than to fail to set a goal at all.

Setting goals is important. If your youth program has no goals, it will:

☐ cover too much ground
☐ major in the minors
☐ have a tendency to ramble
☐ not be related to life needs
☐ have few or no results

Goals are needed for efficiency. Be sure you have specific goals at committee meetings to get the task done. Goals are important so you don't get lost from one youth meeting to the next.

Young people like to follow someone who knows where he is going. Let them see your goals and plans.

Goals are motivators. They help us get going each day. Goals give life purpose and direction. They bring the future into the present. They help us realize our dreams.

Plan for long-range and short-range goals. Long-range goals should reflect the larger vision, while short-range goals cater to specifics.

The Long and the Short of It

Our long-range goal is clearly stated in Scripture. "Like arrows in the hands of a warrior are sons born in one's youth" (Psalm 127:4). You don't shoot an arrow in just any direction; you aim it at a specific target. If young people are like arrows, then we must have a specific goal toward which we are shooting them.

The ultimate goal is "that we may present everyone perfect [mature, complete, whole] in Christ" (Colossians 1:28) and "to prepare God's people for works of service [ministry], so that the body of Christ may be built up" (Ephesians 4:12). Every activity must be considered in light of these verses.

Ask, "Will this activity bring young people to maturity in Christ and prepare them for ministry?" If it won't, then it should be scratched. Whatever you win youth with is what you win them to.

Our short-range goals will differ from year to year. These goals need to be attainable and yet challenging. They need to be measurable, realistic, and accomplishable. Think through these questions and reevaluate your short-range goals.

1. Can you state your short-range goals verbally?
2. What keeps you awake at night?
3. What do you want--at the gut level?
4. What do you want to see happen in the lives of your students and staff?

MY SHORT-RANGE GOAL IS TO BE A PUNK ROCK STAR.

spiritual growth
Church involvement
planning next session
youth w/closer walk w/God
bonded together - unified
set on purpose & walking

Excuses for Not Setting Goals

I have heard some people quote James 4:13-15 as a reason for not setting goals: "Now listen, you who say, 'Today or tomorrow we will go to this or that city, spend a year there, carry on business and make money.' Why, you do not even know what will happen tomorrow. What is your life? You are a mist that appears for a little while and then vanishes. Instead, you ought to say, 'If it is the Lord's will, we will live and do this or that.'" But this passage does not teach that goal-setting is wrong; it teaches that leaving God out of our goal-setting is the mistake.

The key is to set goals and then remain open to God's guidance. After we set a goal, we must move in that direction, continually seeking God's will and timing by praying and listening to what the Lord wants to say to us. God is faithful to steer and guide us if we really want to do what pleases Him.

The Bible says, "Commit your works to the Lord, and your plans will be established" (Proverbs 16:3, NASB). Your plans may not end up exactly as you had intended, but they will be established.

Plans, Priorities, Flexibility, and Fads

Flexibility in youth work is especially important. Have a plan to meet your goals. But always have an alternate plan.

I have a friend who was planning to show a Christian film to 2,700 high schoolers in St. Louis. Unfortunately, the film did not arrive. More unfortunately, my friend did not have a backup plan. What do you do with 2,700 high schoolers in a large auditorium for two hours? My friend did not have a plan "B." What he did have was chaos!

I am convinced that we have time to do whatever we really desire. Youth workers are expected to perform a wide variety of jobs: program planning, counseling, speaking, driving, ministering on campus, teaching, recruiting, and training. We're also supposed to be skilled in youth culture and youth issues. What a job description! Definite goals are needed to help put all of these into proper perspective.

I can tell a great deal about your goals, values, and priorities by looking at just two items: your calendar and your checkbook. How, where, and when you spend your time and money communicates who and what are important to you.

I have been a youth worker for 18 years. During that time, I have seen many younger youth workers pressured into having short-range goals that are not their own. They feel pressured by youth speakers they hear or books they read.

Every few years a "new" avenue of ministry comes up and everyone is supposed to get involved in it. The area of ministry emphasized is always an important one, and workers are intimidated if they are not involved in this particular kind of ministry. Small group Bible study,

missions, family projects, evangelism, social concern, and discipleship are all important, but a youth worker shouldn't feel pressured into keeping all those plates spinning at once.

Design a balanced program for your group. Set goals, keeping your unique group of young people and your personality in mind. Let your youth members help set some of these short-range goals. Stop chasing the latest fad. It will only lead to frustration. Don't be a sponge soaking up everything you hear. Put a strainer in your brain, and sift through the ideas you hear. If you don't plan your time, someone else will.

Avoid Administrative Hassles

I perform better with goals I have set for myself or voluntarily committed myself to, than with goals others have set for me. I like an element of "ownership" in what's going on. At the same time, I think there is an element of danger when a youth worker has no supervision or accountability.

Most young executives-in-the-making are told what to do for the first 8 or 10 years on the job. They are evaluated quarterly. As they gain more expertise, they begin to assume a discretionary style of work, and are gradually permitted to select their own hours and projects. Yet the average age for those starting out in full-time youth work is 26. And most new youth workers are simply turned loose--given incredible executive privileges that most men and women entering the business world won't get till they are 40!

Most of us are not inner-directed enough or disciplined enough to be able to start living an executive lifestyle in our 20s. The result of this is often disorganization.

If you received no written job description when you started in your present

youth-work capacity, you're probably
frustrated when your ideas of youth
work don't match the ideas of the person(s)
to whom you're accountable. Before you
waste any more time trying to merge two or
more different philosophies of youth work,
request a meeting with those to whom you
are responsible. Discuss the various
concepts you all hold. Come to a workable
agreement. Then get the agreed-on job
description in writing so you can get on
with your work instead of using most of
your time and energy in administrative
hassles.

Help
from the
Twilight Zone

One final caution about your goals:
Make sure you keep them in front of you.
If you ever get caught up in the lure of
the past--regardless of your previous suc-
cesses or fond memories--you're destined
for trouble. I can identify with Martin
Sloan, the central character in an old
"Twilight Zone" episode titled "Walking
Distance." At 36, Martin was the vice
president of an ad agency. He appeared to
be successful, but in reality was a burned-
out, exhausted man.

The story line was a simple one. Martin decides to visit Homewood, the town
where he grew up. But when he arrives, he
discovers that he has somehow gone back in
time to when he was a child. He confronts
his parents, but succeeds only in convinc-
ing them he is a lunatic. And when he sees
himself as a child and tries to tell young
Martin to savor his youth, the frightened
boy falls off a merry-go-round and breaks
his leg.

Meanwhile, Martin's father goes through
Martin's wallet, discovers Martin is indeed
his son, and tells Martin to leave because
there is "only one summer to every customer." Martin reluctantly returns to the
present--with a limp he received from
falling off a merry-go-round as a child.

DON'T YOU JUST HATE IT WHEN THE STEWARDSHIP CHAIRMAN PRESENTS HIS ANNUAL GOALS?

The scene near the end of the show between Martin and his father is one that has stuck with me. (Dialogue is from The Twilight Zone Companion, Marc Scott Zicree, Bantam.)

Father: Martin, you have to leave here. There's no room; there's no place. Do you understand that?

Martin: I see that now, but I don't understand. Why not?

Father: I guess because we only get one chance. Maybe there's only one summer to every customer. That little boy, the one I know, the one who belongs here, this is his summer, just as it was yours once--don't make him share it.

Martin: [Bitterly]: All right!

Father: Martin, is it so bad where you're from?

Martin: I thought so, Pop. I've been living at a dead run and I was tired. Then one day, I knew I had to come back here. I had to come back and get on a merry-go-round and eat cotton candy and listen to a band concert, to stop and breathe and close my eyes and smell and listen.

Father: I guess we all want that. Maybe when you go back, Martin, you'll find that there are merry-go-rounds and band concerts where you are. Maybe you haven't been looking in the right place. You've been looking behind you, Martin. Try looking ahead.

I hope this book will help you learn to free up enough time to recognize the merry-go-rounds, band concerts, and cotton candy that are here now. I pray that because of this book, you'll find new ways to get things done and to enjoy your family, your ministry, and your quiet times with God. And as good as the past may have been for you, I urge you to set goals and establish priorities that will make your future even better.

planning calendar for Sun eve programs
set aside time for reading
clean desk
more budget
limit trips to store

contact friends more
eat + exercise more
work less
enjoy diff activities
train others to handle responsibilities

Time to Respond

1. Review your calendar and your check-book. Where do they indicate you spend most of your time and money?

    Church
    Lakeland

2. Are you satisfied with the priorities you've set for your time and your money? What changes would you make, if any?

3. What changes would you make in your life if you knew you only had one year to live? What if you had 50 more years? Why?

4. Are you trying to minister to the young people in the church, or to those outside the church? What percent of your time is spent in discipleship? In evangelism? In social concern?

5. What are your short-range goals for this year? What are your long-range goals?

6. To whom are you accountable? With whom do you share your victories and defeats?

7. Do you have a job description? If not, why not?

    I never wrote one

Someone has said, "What you're doing speaks so loudly I can't hear what you're saying." Setting goals and talking about your priorities is one thing. But working toward your goals and sticking to your priorities is another.

This chapter contains several timesaving ideas to help you put into practice the goals and priorities you have set. I share them from my personal experience, because they have worked well for me. You may need to adapt some of them to fit your specific ministry, but the principles behind each method listed have been proven effective. Please don't file these suggestions in the section of your mind labeled, "Theory that sounds good." Use them! Practice them! Let them work for you!

Work Smarter, Not Harder

My dad taught me the principle of working smarter instead of harder while I was still a child. For instance, when my bicycle had a flat tire and I was taking the wheel off in the grass at night, he would suggest ways to improve the repair process. I soon learned to do the work during the day (when I could see what I was doing), on the sidewalk (so I wouldn't lose important parts), and without having to take off the wheel (so I would save time). Now as a youth worker, when I need to "fix a flat," I immediately look for more efficient ways to accomplish my tasks.

I am not suggesting that God honors laziness. Throughout Scripture we are told to work and not be lazy. (See, for instance, Proverbs 6:10; 18:9; 19:24; 21:25; 26:13-15.) But more of us need to learn to use our time produc-tively.

I know a lot of disorganized youth workers who tell me, "I gotta hurry. What if Jesus comes back tomorrow?" My response is, "What if He doesn't come back for

TIME-SAVERS

CHAPTER THREE

WORK SMARTER, NOT HARDER! WHY DIDN'T I THINK OF THAT BEFORE?

1,000 years?" The work we do should have lasting results, not merely "put out fires" as they arise.

One way that many of today's youth workers are working "smarter" is by using modern technology such as personal computers. A computer is an excellent tool for sermon preparation, putting together a youth directory, all kinds of record-keeping, and endless other recurring chores. Another helpful tool is a variable speed cassette recorder. You can learn to understand what the speaker is saying at twice the speed, and cut listening time in half. Be on the lookout for innovative ways you can work smarter (not harder) in your youth work.

Double Your Time

Look for opportunities to complete two tasks in the time it usually takes to complete one. For example:

- [ ] While driving or working in the garage, you can listen to tapes (music or sermons), pray, dictate letters, practice speeches, memorize Scripture, or talk to someone.

- [ ] Instead of thumbing through three-year-old magazines at a doctor's, dentist's, or optometrist's office, take a book to read, some letters to write, or some other constructive activity to complete.

- [ ] Combine lunch and business when you can. Take someone to lunch who wants to meet with you, or better yet, get him to take you to lunch.

- [ ] Let your mind "work on" something right before you go to sleep. Who knows? You might get a great idea during the night. (On Saturday night I always try to review the Sunday School lesson I am to teach the next day. Then I am ready to "go for it" on Sunday morning.)

Think about the activities you are involved in. Where can you double up and do two things at once? Try it. Then use the extra time in a different constructive activity.

Share the "Blessing"

Lone-Ranger-type youth workers are ineffective. Oh, sure, they become the gurus of the groups they oversee. They stay in the spotlight on center stage. They get plenty of applause. But they accomplish little for the Lord if they try to do all the jobs themselves. Eventually they burn out.

At one point in his life, Moses was a prime candidate for burnout. He was the only judge for all of Israel, and was working from morning till night. Fortunately, Moses took the wise advice of his father-in-law, Jethro. He delegated the smaller decisions to other capable people and only tackled the most difficult cases himself. (See Exodus 18:13-27.)

Once a youth worker learns to delegate, he is relieved of the pressure that accumulates from hundreds of tiny chores that always need to be done. He can then concentrate on spending more time with the young people in his group.

But be aware of two warnings as you learn to delegate. First, don't expect the work to be done exactly as you would have done it yourself. As long as the results are similar to those you would have reached, be content with an adequate job.

Second, don't allow your volunteers to feel like they are pawns in another person's program. They will feel pleased to know that they are being used by God, but not so pleased if they think they are being used by you. Make sure they know that they are part of a team. If other adults see that you genuinely need and value their contributions, you should have

THIS IS THE LAST TIME I DELEGATE TRANSPORTATION TO SOMEONE ELSE.

little trouble finding additional youth workers.

Learn to Say No

I am convinced that the most difficult word for youth workers to pronounce is not Zaanannim (Joshua 19:33) or Hazzelelponi (1 Chronicles 4:3). This word is even harder to say than, "The sixth sick sheik's sixth sheep's sick." The word, in case you haven't already guessed, is "no."

Charles Spurgeon said, "Learn to say no; it will be more use to you than to be able to read Latin." Why? Because when you don't say no you wind up making promises you can't keep, going to meetings you don't really need to attend, and wasting time in hundreds of other non-productive activities.

Saying no doesn't come easily for several reasons. The most obvious reason is probably that we want people to like us, so we tell them what they want to hear. We often go to great lengths to prevent the possibility of someone becoming upset with us.

Other times we say yes because a matter seems to be "urgent." Yet while we attend to the "urgent," the really important activities don't get done. I can truthfully say that during the past 18 years of my work with youth there have been very few legitimate "urgent" crises that demanded my attention immediately. General Eisenhower said, "The more important an item, the less likely that it is urgent. The more urgent an item, the less likely that it is important."

A third reason that many of us say no so infrequently is because of the common youth worker's attitude that he is indispensable. Be honest. How often have you thought to yourself, "If I don't do it, nobody else will"? Or, "If I were to leave, this place would fall apart"?

Garbage! If you say no and God doesn't
provide someone else to do the job, maybe
He doesn't want it done at all. In fact,
if you say yes when you ought to say no,
you are actually depriving another person
of the chance to serve. Don't let
your pride and ego get in the way. None
of us is indispensable.

Don't be afraid to discontinue a
project if it is going nowhere. Make a
motion to adjourn a meeting that is
obviously nonproductive. Step back,
evaluate and analyze what is causing the
problems, and start again. Learning to
say no isn't easy, but it must be done if
you are serious about learning to manage
your time effectively.

Every time I say no to one thing, I am
saying yes to something else. So the key
is to feel good about the things I am
saying yes to and not bad about the
things I say no to.

When Jesus Said No

Jesus said no to the following:

HUMAN REQUESTS
    Let me bury my father before I follow You   Matthew 8:21-22
    Tell my sister to help me with housework   Luke 10:38-42
    Stay in our town a little longer   Luke 4:42-44

FRIENDS WHO ASKED FAVORS
    Give my sons a privileged place next to You   Matthew 20:20-23
    Stop talking about Your death like that   Mark 8:31-38
    Tell us when the last things will occur   Acts 1:6-7
    Call down fire to destroy towns that reject You   Luke 9:54-56

DEMANDS OF THE CROWDS
    Work a sign for us here and now   Matthew 12:38-45
    Do here in Your own town the things we have
        heard You did in Capernaum   Luke 4:23-24
    Give us again today the bread You gave us yesterday   John 6:41-58

COMMON SENSE, LAW-AND-ORDER, CITIZENS' REQUESTS
    Send the crowd away; they're getting hungry   Luke 9:12-17
    Keep this crowd quiet   Luke 19:37-40
    Make Your followers fast like John the Baptist   Mark 2:18-22
    Answer the accusations against You   Mark 15:4-5

(Rev. George Niederauer, "When Jesus Said No," The Priest, December, 1978)

Use a Things-to-Do List

Mr. Ivy Lee was a time management consultant who once presented Charles Schwab, former president of Bethlehem Steel, with a proposal he thought would save Mr. Schwab some time. He asked Schwab to try it for three months and then mail him a check for what he thought the idea was worth. Three months later Mr. Lee received a check for $35,000.

Mr. Lee's idea was so simple, you may be tempted to skip right over this section. Don't! The suggestion that was worth $35,000 to Mr. Schwab was to use a daily list of things that need doing, and to do them in order of priority.

If _you_ don't plan your day, someone else will. A things-to-do list keeps your essential activities in front of you until they get done. It keeps your energy channeled into significant tasks instead of allowing time to slip away on trivial matters.

You may be tempted to just list tomorrow's things to do in your head, but it is _essential_ to put them on paper. Then stick to your list and don't get sidetracked by extraneous things. And don't get overzealous and write down 23 things to do, or you are likely to become frustrated and not accomplish anything.

Back-dating is helpful as you put together your daily things-to-do list. When you are planning a big event in the future, you can work backward and establish priorities for each action that must be taken to prepare for the event. You wouldn't want to write, "Plan 5-day bicycle trip," because that in itself could take all week. Instead, break it down into smaller, achievable activities: arrange for publicity, plan menu, find transportation, request cooks, prepare devotions, schedule practice rides, etc. Define all tasks specifically. "Study history" is not as measurable as, "Read

WHAT DO YOU MEAN, "FILING SYSTEM"? THIS IS YOUR THINGS-TO-DO LIST.

chapter 8." Definable tasks make it easier
to recognize when you are finished with
them.

I find it helpful to group the activities on my things-to-do list. I make all
my telephone calls at the same time. I
schedule another block of time for writing
letters. I tackle one thing and work on
it till it's finished. Then comes the best
part: I grab a bold red felt-tip pen,
check off the item just completed, and
let out with a loud "HaaYaa!" sound--some-
what like Miss Piggy's karate scream. Try
it sometime. It feels great to know
you have finished something. (And don't
forget the "HaaYaa!") Then reward yourself. Take yourself out for a Coke or
watch a favorite TV show.

Carve Out Uninterrupted Time

I don't know how many times I've been
"on a roll" working on a message only to
have someone stick his head in my office
and ask, "Can I have just 30 seconds?"
To the person asking, 30 seconds is a
small request. But to me, that 30
seconds stretches into 15 or 20 minutes
after the person is gone as I try to get
back into writing. Interruptions can
derail some great thoughts, so I have
devised several ways to avoid disruptive
breaks in my work time.

- ☐ My office hours begin at 9 a.m. But
  my unofficial arrival time (which
  only a few people know) is 8:15 a.m.
  I can get a lot done in the 45
  minutes when I am undisturbed by
  phones or people.
- ☐ I also use a "do not disturb" sign on
  my door. Or if I really want to
  guard my thinking time, I hold the
  sign in front of my chest as I walk
  through the church halls. The sign
  tells others that I don't want to be
  interrupted for anything less than a
  nuclear attack.

□ I have learned to hide. When under
pressure, I often escape to a public
library, a park bench, or a room in
the church that no one else is using.
In an emergency, I might even check
into a motel for a night where phones
won't be ringing, people won't be
dropping by, and staff members won't
be around to make requests.

Youth ministry is built around people
and led by people. Learn to work well
with the people around you. But don't
hesitate to take an occasional break from
those people to refresh your spirit. It
will do you--and them--a world of good.

Get Organized

Stationery stores contain dozens of nicely
packaged filing systems, but most of them
are too complicated and require too much
paper shuffling. My files (in manila
folders) contain only six major sections:

(1) Letters folder (copies of letters
    I've sent)
(2) Publicity folder (previous publicity
    mailings)
(3) Bible studies section (one folder
    for each study, filed alphabetically
    so each can be easily found and
    added to at a later date)
(4) Illustrations folder
(5) Maps folder (directions to camps,
    retreat centers, amusement parks,
    beach, homes, stores, airports,
    etc.)
(6) Activities section (one folder for
    each activity--graduation programs,
    stewardship banquet, camps, new-
    member classes, youth choir tours,
    etc.)

Within easy reach on my desk I keep a
master calendar, a folder on visitation
calls to make, a speaking engagement
folder, a folder on upcoming Bible studies,
and a couple of folders for specific
activities I am working on that week.
Your filing system will no doubt be a

little different, but streamline it
wherever possible and you might be surprised at the time you can save.

Count
on Your Calendar

John Wesley once said, "Though I am always
in haste, I am never in a hurry, because I
never undertake more work than I can go
through with calmness of spirit." Most
youth workers are "always in haste," but I
know very few who have "calmness of
spirit." Many of them could benefit from
the proper use of a calendar.

A lot of the youth leaders I know have
two or three calendars--one at home, one
at the office, and perhaps another one to
carry around in their pockets, cars, or
purses. But problems arise when they
schedule conflicting appointments or
neglect to record important meetings on
all of the calendars.

I recommend having just one master
calendar to keep in your office. I
prefer the 8 1/2" x 11" size that shows me
a month at a glance and also has plenty of
room in which to write. A master calendar
gives me time to think about requests
before acting. If someone asks me to do
something, I have them write it down, and
then I tell them I have to check my master
calendar. That way I have time to evaluate
those requests in light of my ministry
goals and other obligations.

Don't Get Lost
in the Mail

Last year I received some junk mail from
an insurance company that had a skull and
crossbones on the envelope beneath
which was written, "WARNING, if you throw
this into your wastebasket unopened, a
capsule of water inside will break,
spilling onto a dehydrated boa constrictor.
He will then crawl out and crush your
little body." I liked the idea so much

that I used it for one of our youth mailings. Unfortunately, most junk mail is just a waste of time.

Learn to toss junk mail. In fact, make an art of it. Practice tossing unopened junk mail into the garbage can like throwing cards into a hat. Or another option is to be like a guy I know who tries to get on every mailing list he can find. He receives hundreds of pieces of junk mail every day, rolls them into fireplace logs, and gets through the winter without having to buy wood.

I believe in handling letters as little as possible. I used to open a letter, read it, say to myself, "I'll have to write back," and put it in a pile of things to be done. Sometimes I would read the letter five or six times before answering, and other times the letter would get lost. Now when I open a letter, I answer it immediately if at all possible. I owe no one a letter. It's a great feeling to never get behind in letter writing.

Another timesaver for me is to answer a letter by writing my response on the bottom of it. Then I just put it in another envelope and send it off the same day. Of course, I don't do that with all my mail, but it's OK for a lot of my correspondence.

You may be able to save time and money by using the phone instead of writing a letter. But be aware of the possible hazards of telephone use. (See the section that follows.)

Telephone: Friend or Foe?

I have never gotten along well with telephones. They have interrupted my dinners, stolen my dimes, and fallen apart in my hands. I am not fond of busy signals, unlisted numbers, answering machines, long-distance dialing, or solicitors who just won't quit.

If you use a things-to-do list, the telephone probably will not dictate your day. If you don't, watch out. You are at the mercy of anyone who decides to call. If you have a secretary, make sure he or she screens your calls whenever possible so you only have to stop for the most pressing matters. You can get back to the other callers when it is more convenient.

Telephone answering machines can be either a blessing or a curse. With a machine, you won't miss your important calls, but you won't miss the unimportant ones either. You'll probably have to get back to a lot of people who could have found out what they needed to know from someone else if your recorded message wasn't so easy to respond to.

An answering machine can become a time waster if you're like a lot of people I know who spend half their day trying to think of clever messages to put on them. And sometimes the machines self-destruct and you don't get a clear message when you play them back. Nothing would be worse than hearing, "Les, I am about to commit suicide. Please help. My number is 555-mppphh."

You probably know most of the ways a phone can be a timesaver, but the methods are worth repeating "just in case."

- Keep paper and a functional pen or pencil close to the telephone.
- Have emergency and often-used numbers next to your phone so you won't have to look them up every time.
- Use the phone (instead of driving) to locate needed materials, order take-out food, make reservations, and take care of other routine matters.
- Always repeat important messages on the telephone. You will save a lot of hassles later.
- Write down what you want to say in outline form before calling. (When Gretchen and I were dating, I would call her and say, "I need to talk to you about four things. First . . . ." I may not have been very romantic, but I never left anything out.)

I'M SORRY, THE YOUTH PASTOR CAN'T COME TO THE PHONE AGAIN. HE'S IN THE BACK YARD TRYING TO THROW A ROPE OVER THE LIMB OF A TALL TREE.

I THINK THE YOUTH MINISTER JUST STARTED DINNER. LET'S PUT THOSE CALLS THROUGH NOW. HEE! HEE!

The telephone can destroy a youth worker's family. It can become your master if you willingly become its slave. Don't hesitate to turn it off or unplug it during meals and family times. If someone needs to get in touch with you, he will call back later.

Keys to Remembering

How many times have you arrived at your office only to discover that you left something you need at home? The return trip is all wasted time, so I use my keys as reminders when I need to take something to work. If I put my keys on top of the things I need or on an important note reminding me to do something, I am much less likely to forget what I am supposed to do.

Do the Write Thing

Sundays are busy days for every youth worker (unless you're a Seventh Day Adventist). I usually confront a barrage of young people and parents in the church halls on Sunday who want to meet with me at a specific time during the week. Years ago I tried to rely on my memory to keep those appointments straight. But if too many people talked to me before I reached my office, I would get the names, dates, and times all confused.

Now when someone wants me to do something for them, I always have them write it down on a piece of paper. At the end of the day I pull out all the pieces of paper and put the requests on my things-to-do list and master calendar. If I accidentally schedule two appointments for the same time, I call one of the persons and set up a different day or time. But such conflicts are rare.

I also write down a brilliant idea as soon as I think of it (about once a year,

I PUT MY KEYS ON TOP OF THE LUGGAGE SO I WOULD REMEMBER IT, MADAM, BUT I SEEM TO HAVE FORGOTTEN THE CAR...

if I'm lucky). If I don't write it down, I never remember it. I may wake up in the middle of the night with a solution to a problem I have been working on for weeks, and I write it down.   But if you try this idea, keep a flashlight by the bed. I must confess that some mornings I wake up to read something like, "A great illustration for the message on God's forgiveness is the story of siggle and mphf or muggle all cobsko ugglephmps???"

Get Some Much-needed Help

Without a doubt the second-greatest help in time management (losing out only to the things-to-do list) is a secretary. If you don't have one, try to convince your church or organization to hire one for a few hours each week, or see if someone is willing to volunteer.

   My secretary has become indispensable to me. A few of the responsibilities she has been able to assume over the years include:

- ☐ Keeping mailing lists accurate and sending out mailings for junior high through college
- ☐ Typing messages, sermons, lists, letters, memos, etc.
- ☐ Alphabetizing lists
- ☐ Greeting guests
- ☐ Laying out publicity pieces
- ☐ Registering people for camps and conferences
- ☐ Answering the telephone
- ☐ Keeping records
- ☐ Typing articles for our weekly newspaper
- ☐ Making telephone calls
- ☐ Running errands
- ☐ Making airline and hotel reservations

   Again, specific responsibilities will vary from church to church. But begin to look for things you do that could be handled just as capably (or more capably) by a secretary, and then find one who is willing to do the job.

STAFF DESCRIPTIONS

SENIOR MINISTER
Able to leap tall buildings in a single bound;
Is more powerful than a locomotive;
Is faster than a speeding bullet;
Walks on water;
Gives policies to God.

ASSOCIATE MINISTER
Is able to leap short buildings in a single bound;
Is as powerful as a switch engine;
Is just as fast as a speeding bullet;
Walks on water if the sea is calm.
Talks with God.

EDUCATIONAL DIRECTOR
Leaps short buildings with a running start;
Is almost as powerful as a switch engine;
Is faster than a speeding BB;
Walks on water if he knows where stumps are;
Talks with God if special request is approved.

MUSIC DIRECTOR
Clears a quonset hut;
Loses race with a locomotive;
Can fire a speeding bullet;
Swims well;
Is occasionally addressed by God.

YOUTH DIRECTOR
Runs into small building;
Recognizes locomotives two out of three times;
Used a squirt gun in college;
Knows how to use the water fountain;
Mumbles to himself.

CHURCH SECRETARY
Lifts buildings to walk under them;
Kicks locomotives off the track;
Catches speeding bullets with her teeth;
Freezes water with a single glance;
When God speaks, she says, "May I ask who's calling?"

Use Your Common Sense

Obviously, the suggestions listed in this chapter are not a complete list of time-saving ideas. No matter how smoothly your system is working, you can probably come up with another improvement or two. Look around you. What things are you doing that could be done in less time? Don't overlook those things you do automatically --without thinking. Often those are the activities that are subtly stealing away your precious time.

The purpose of the time-savers in this chapter is to help you do your work more effectively--not necessarily to provide time for you to do more work. This chapter has only suggested ways to squeeze some additional time out of a busy schedule. The next chapter will give you some direction in how you might want to use some of that time you're saving.

SORRY, DEAR. THIS ISN'T NEXT ON MY THINGS-TO-DO-LIST.

Time to Respond

block time *up coming act*
evaluate needed *break down time*
schedule

library

1. What shortcuts can you take to work smarter, not harder?

2. What events of your day are potential times to double your time (driving to work, mowing the lawn, etc.)? What things can you do during those activities to double your time?

3. What are you involved in now that you should have avoided by saying no? Why didn't you say no to those tasks?

4. What programs or activities take excessive time and energy and produce few results? What might happen if you stop them and try something different?

5. What jobs can you delegate to others?

6. What responsibilities could a secretary handle for you? If you have a secretary, when was the last time you told your secretary--in word or deed--how valuable he/she is to you?

7. Where are some good places away from the office for you to get work done?

8. How long has it been since you've cleaned out your desk and office/work space to get rid of junk and to file anything you want to keep?

9. How can you synchronize your calendars if you have more than one? Do you have a secretary or friend who could help you do this?

10. Where can you keep your keys to help you remember things?

11. Do you have a notepad or pieces of paper and a small pen in all of your jackets or purses so you can jot down ideas and appointments you need to remember?

12. What is on your things-to-do list for tomorrow?

TIME MANAGE-MENT: WHY BOTHER?

CHAPTER FOUR

HONEY, YOU'VE GOT TO STOP BRINGING WORK HOME FROM THE OFFICE!

A number of youth ministers enjoy the spinning-plates syndrome, and seem to thrive on a harried pace. They may grumble, but inside they really enjoy it. Maybe they like hard work. Or maybe they're workaholics.

A workaholic is addicted to work in the same way an alcoholic is addicted to drink. Work is the workaholic's idol. When he <u>does</u> take a day off, work is still on his mind. He takes job-related books on vacation. Each day he takes work home with him, even if he doesn't touch it. Antacid manufacturers love this person.

I believe strongly in hard work and long hours. But some youth workers have gone to such an extreme that they use work as an escape from life. We need to check our motives for working and our attitudes in regard to our jobs and lives. How can we lead young people into quiet places beside still waters if we're in perpetual motion?

If you can't find a 24-hour period to rest in a normal week, either your job is poorly defined and you are required to work too hard for a living, or you are not organizing your workload. If youth workers never learn to manage time, they can easily work 24 hours a day, 7 days a week, 52 weeks a year. There is always something else to tackle.

Who hasn't felt guilty about the imperfection of a message he has given? Or a program, activity, or counseling session that has apparently bombed? I remember pounding the steering wheel after a Bible study, thinking I could have done at least 50 percent better presenting the material. I felt that I'd cheated those kids. Youth workers suffer from an addiction to perfection, but in reality perfectionists produce little more than dreams. Sometimes we have to sacrifice perfection for simply getting things done well and on time.

Youth workers are easy targets for the workaholic bug. They feel that no one notices what they are doing, so they become more aggressive. They work longer hours, competing with everyone on every level.

These workaholics feel "driven" by an intoxicating need to achieve in order to be accepted. A lot of times they feel inadequate. They often use work as an excuse for not getting close to people. James D. Berkley said, "[Workaholics] function poorly, are ineffective, out of step, miserable. I often marvel at their perseverance and shudder at the price they and their churches pay."

Make Time for Yourself

It's not hard to understand why so many youth workers develop workaholic attitudes. Partially to blame are the conditions under which we have to work. Youth workers are not confined to an office from 8:00 to 5:00, so they are never quite certain when they're "on duty" or "off duty." Many times they have little close personal supervision. They often structure their own time. This occasionally results in a youth worker becoming lazy. But most of the time the opposite is true.

Many youth workers never take any time for themselves. Most tend to be hyper-active and feel guilty when they take a day off. Eugene C. Kennedy said, "Leisure is still a monstrous puzzle for everyone nurtured on the Protestant work ethic" (William T. McConnell, The Gift of Time, InterVarsity, p. 31).

The Lord once called His disciples together and gave them power to go minister to those in need. The disciples returned and shared with Jesus all they had done (Luke 9:10). When they finished talking, Jesus didn't tell them to hit the sack and get at it again in the morning. In-stead, Jesus quietly slipped away with them toward the city of Bethsaida for some well deserved R & R (rest and relaxation).

YOUTH GROUP BUNCH OF ANIMALS. ME GO FAR AWAY.

If you want to be effective in youth work you <u>must</u> set aside time for yourself. Personal <u>time</u> must be given the same priority as professional time. Block it out on your calendar.

After a long weekend retreat where you have been working three straight days and nights, take a half day off for relaxation. If you have a large activity that will require you to be alert for a lengthy period of time, take a half day off before the activity. Check your calendar to see if you've planned adequate rest times. Use some of this time to think, pray, and read your Bible.

Consider taking one day a month to be alone. Get involved in a favorite hobby that will refresh you. Take time to read some books that will be of interest to you <u>personally</u> and not just for your ministry. Make <u>your</u> personal day something to look forward to.

In the years when I was in high school, youth leaders often asked young people, "If Jesus were to come back right now, would you want Him to find you doing something that's not worthwhile?" That question helped many kids think through questionable activities. But, unfortunately, that attitude also caused many people to feel guilty for taking time off to play racquetball, ride a bicycle, or, worse yet, play Uno. It's easy to forget that God rested (Genesis 2:3) and wants us to rest (Matthew 11:29; Psalm 116:7).

Take some time to be with friends who can minister to <u>you.</u> (I like to play Monopoly with guys who are not involved in my ministry.) Plan to occasionally relax and just goof off. Active exercise such as jogging, bicycling, handball, swimming, or tennis will help you leave your worries at the office--for a while, at least.

Nobody is going to order you to take time for yourself. Unless <u>you</u> plan to relax, you will burn yourself out and become useless to the kids that God has put under your care. Stay in control of your job. Don't let the job control you.

Make Time for Your Family

The youth worker himself is only the first victim of his workaholic tendencies. The members of his family also suffer. James Dobson said it well: "Overcommitment is the greatest foe to the stable Christian family . . . because we don't manage our time." Your family needs to be a high priority in your ministry.

The average father, according to most surveys, spends 30 seconds a day with his preschool children. Can you believe that? I heard one father respond to that statistic, "Thirty seconds may not be a lot of time with my kids, but the time we spend is quality time." That's a bunch of garbage, rubbish, sewage, and dung. (My Christian convictions prevent stronger language.)

Spend a quantity of time as well as quality time alone with your kids. Take them places with you. And don't treat your time with them like another appointment in your busy schedule. The best times to talk to your kids are when you're kicking back on the patio with a Coke in your hand, and they know you're not going somewhere in an hour.

Don't try to vacation at home. The phone still rings, and you always end up at the office "just for a couple of minutes." Get away and have a great time.

Don't take every speaking engagement you are offered. It may be great for your ego, but it's hard on your family. If I know that a preacher is the father of young children, I don't get too excited when I hear him bragging about being gone each year on a 30-week speaking tour.

In a survey of hundreds of children, family life specialist Delmer W. Holbrook came up with three things fathers say most in response to their kids. "I'm too tired" takes first place. "We don't have enough money" is second. And "Keep quiet" is third.

Possibly the saddest statement I have ever read was made by evangelist Billy Sunday: "The tragedy of my life is that although I've led thousands of people to Jesus Christ, my own sons are not saved" (Leadership, Fall, 1981, p. 107). But an equally encouraging statement comes from Francis Quarles: "In early life I had nearly been betrayed into the principles of spiritual infidelity, but there was one argument in favor of Christianity that I could not refute, and that was the consistent character and example of my own father."

Put your children's significant events (birthdays, ball games, music recitals, school plays) on your calendar before less important things crowd them out. Special family times (family nights, outings, holidays, anniversaries, relatives' birthdays) should go on the calendar also. Traditions create and reinforce emotional security in the home. They give stability to the family. Special days help us to pause and reflect on life.

Use travel times for conversations, games, and songs. Use mealtimes for discussions, jokes, riddles, and to discuss events of the day. Use bedtimes for physical closeness, stories, and prayer.

We have all heard, "The family that prays together stays together." I'd like to change that statement to read, "The family that plays together stays together." Praying together comes out of playing together. A Christian home should be the most fun place on the block.

Be creative. For instance, we don't have any furniture in our living room because we often have youth groups over to our house. But when the youth groups don't meet here, my family usually has a camping tent set up in the middle of the living room. It looks a little strange to the neighbors, but not to us. We go camping in the living room every few weeks. We bring out folding chairs, sit outside the tent, and talk. Then we sleep

in our sleeping bags inside the tent.
It's a great time together and our two
preschool boys love it.

Make Time
for Your Spouse

Take time to be alone with your spouse
as well. Eat out together at least once a
week, even if you only go to McDonald's.
Get away overnight together every couple
of months. Leave on Friday afternoon,
find a motel a few miles away, and
return on Saturday afternoon. Hide
encouraging notes for each other around
the house under the lid of the washing
machine or in the refrigerator.

And make sure you leave the pressures
of your work at work; don't take them
home with you. I have a friend named
Shirley who works for the court system in
Orange County, California. She heads a
staff that takes care of children who are
child abuse and incest victims. (Orange
County had 742 reported cases of incest
in 1983.)

When I asked Shirley how working in
this kind of environment affects her home
life and family, she gave me an extremely
helpful insight. She told me that as she
walks to her door each evening, she dumps
all her frustrations, anger, and fears from
work on a large bush outside her house. In
the morning when she leaves she picks them
back up again.

As a youth worker you are in a giving
ministry, but you can't afford to give
everything you've got to the "kids" at
work and overlook your own kids at home.
Talk to your spouse and see if he or she
thinks you're too caught up in your work.
And take action now to correct any problems you discover. Don't wait till it's
too late.

The following letter came to my desk
about 10 years ago. It recounts tragedy,
but it has been a reminder to me over
the years to keep my priorities straight.

Diary of a Mad Housewife

My husband is a full-time youth director. He is extremely dedicated and spends between 50 and 70 hours a week with young people. I think the reason he is so successful with kids is that he is always available to them, always ready to help when they need him.

That may be why the attendance has more than doubled in the past year. He really knows how to talk their language. This past year he would be out two and three nights a week talking with kids till midnight. He's always taking them to camps and ski trips and overnight camp-outs. If he isn't with kids, he's thinking about them and preparing for his next encounter with them.

And if he has any time left after that, he is speaking or attending a conference where he can share with others what God is doing through him. When it comes to youth work, my husband has always been 100 percent.

I guess that's why I left him.

There isn't much left after 100 percent. Frankly, I just could not compete with "God." I say that because my husband always had a way of reminding me that this was God's work, and he must minister where and when God called him. Young people today desperately need help and God had called him to help them. When a young person needed him, he had to respond or he would be letting God and the young person down.

When I did ask my husband to spend some time with the kids or me, it was always tentative and if I became pushy about it I was "nagging," "trying to get him out of God's work," "behaving selfishly," or I was revealing a "spiritual problem."

Honestly, I have never wanted anything but God's will for my husband, but I never could get him to consider that maybe his family was part of that will.

It didn't matter how many "discussions" we had about his schedule, he would always end with, "OK, I'll get out of the ministry, if that's what you want." Of course, I didn't want that, so we would continue as always until another "discussion."

You can ask for only so long. There is a limit to how long you can be ignored and put off. You threaten to leave without meaning it till you keep the threat. You consider all the unpleasant consequences till they don't seem unpleasant anymore. You decide that nothing could be more unpleasant than being alone, feeling worthless.

You finally make up your mind that you are a person with real worth as an individual. You assert your ego and join womanhood again. That's what I did. I wanted to be more than housekeeper, diaper changer, and sex partner.

I wanted to be free from the deep bitterness and guilt that slowly ate at my spiritual and psychological sanity. Deep inside there was something making me not only dislike my husband, but everything he did or touched.

His "I love you" became meaningless to me because he didn't act like it.

His gifts were evidence to me of his <u>guilt</u> because he didn't spend more time with me. His sexual advances were met with a frigidity that frustrated both of us and deepened the gap between us.

All I wanted was to feel as though he really wanted to be with me. But, no matter how hard I tried, I always felt like I was keeping him from something. He had a way of making me feel guilty because I had forced him to spend his valuable time with the kids and myself. Just once I wish he would have canceled something for us instead of canceling us.

You don't have to believe this, but I really loved him and his ministry once. I never wanted him to work an eight-to-five job. Nor did I expect him to be home every night. I tried to believe every promise he made me, honestly hoping things would change, but they never did.

All of a sudden I woke up one day and realized that I had become a terribly bitter person. I not only resented my husband and his work, but I was beginning to despise myself. In desperation to save myself, our children and, I guess, even my husband and his ministry, I left him.

I don't think he really believed I'd leave him. I guess I never really believed I'd leave him either.

But I did!

("Diary of a Mad Housewife,"
<u>The Wittenburg Door</u>, June, 1971, p. 8, Youth Specialties)

SLIPPING OFF TO ANOTHER YOUTH CONVENTION, DEAR?

Failed Successes

What can make a hard-working, conscientious youth worker lose all perspective and begin to take for granted the people who should mean the most to him? What causes his priorities to get out of line? What evolves good Christian leaders into misguided workaholics? I think the source of these problems is an incorrect emphasis on or understanding of success.

How do you evaluate success in youth ministry? The most common answer I hear is "attendance." Possibly the most-asked question at youth leaders' conferences is: "How many do you have in your group?"

I honestly believe attendance is important. The early church was a growing church reaching out to the world. But I don't think attendance is necessarily the best criteria for measuring success. Anyone can attract a large crowd. The question is, why are they coming?

Attendance can fluctuate in youth work no matter how you plan. Some years you get a flaky, lethargic class that's going nowhere, and attendance drops. A couple of years later a dynamite, aggressive, evangelistic group comes barreling through and they bring their friends, relatives, neighbors, and pet iguanas. Yet if a youth leader doesn't see an increase in attendance over last year, he feels obligated to "do more."

As the pressure for numerical success grows, so does the subtle desire to sacrifice content for the sake of reaching more young people. It is interesting to note that while church attendance across the country is on the rise, no moral revival is accompanying the numerical growth. The most condemning piece of literature I have read was the statement by George Gallup at the end of a penetrating survey on the religious climate in America. He said, "Never before in the history of the United States has the

Gospel of Jesus Christ made such inroads
while at the same time making so little
difference as to how people live."

Many youth ministers have gone the
world's route in being interested in
symbols: What is your title? How much
power do you have? How much are you paid?
How many people know you exist? Has your
picture been in Group, Campus Life,
Christianity Today, Moody Monthly, or The
Wittenburg Door?

These youth ministers are looking
through the wrong end of the telescope.
Everything they do has to be "bigger" or
"better." They are always looking over
their shoulders, comparing their ministries
with someone else's ministry.

The danger for these success-driven
youth workers is that they begin to use
people rather than develop them. They
tend to invest their time in things that
receive public acclaim, and things that
folks will applaud. Then they become
so blind that they honestly think that
these things are the call of God.

King Saul was a success-driven man.
But he left this life a suicidal person
desperately trying to hold on to his
job, because he couldn't stand to see
anyone else pass him up. Saul was relying
on his natural abilities. He put God in
the backseat.

Each of us has a desire for recognition,
a desire to be important or influential.
Paul calls it the pride of life. It's a
desire to be noticeably superior, and it
explains our winner complexes and our
workaholic natures. We have allowed the
world to impose standards of success
on us that are not biblical.

Vernon C. Grounds in Christianity Today
writes, "[Success] worships the shrine of
sanctified or unsanctified statistics.
We are sinfully concerned about size--the
size of sanctuaries, the size of salaries,
the size of Sunday Schools. We are
sinfully preoccupied with statistics about
budgets and buildings and buses and

baptisms. God's standards of success differ from the world's" ("What's So Great About Success?" December 9, 1977. Used by permission). Jesus affirms that "What is highly valued among men is detestable in God's sight" (Luke 16:15).

When we adapt to the methodology and standards of the world, are we suggesting that Jesus is not enough? Jesus refused to appeal to the baser motives. He needs to be our drawing card.

Successful Failures

Another danger of wanting to succeed (as the world looks at success) is that we become afraid to fail. We don't want to take risks. We begin to play it safe.

We need to realize it's OK to fail. It's healthy to work through a failure and learn from it. It is part of living on the cutting edge. Let's not cheat our-selves out of the growing time that comes only through failure.

Failure helps you discover where your blind and weak spots are. It can push you in a new direction and make you sensitive to the needs of others.

Most Bible colleges fail to prepare graduates for failure. We will not all be Billy Grahams, Robert Schullers, or Mother Teresas. In fact, most of us will work without ever being well known. Remember, Jesus never traveled very far, and gave most of His life to 12 men.

In baseball nobody bats 1.000. The best hitter in American baseball was Ted Williams. He hit over .400 twice in his career. He failed 6 out of every 10 times at bat.

Actor Robert Montgomery captured the world's attitude toward success when he said, "If you achieve success you will get applause. Enjoy it . . . but never quite believe it."

WHO SAYS NO ONE BATS 1.000?

What is success in youth ministry? Let me give you three guidelines that I have been using for 18 years, and hope to use for the rest of my life.

(1) The acid test is to see if the young people I am now working with are still committed to the Lord 20, 30, 40 years from now, or whether their commitment was just a passing fad.

(2) H.G. Wells said it this way: "Wealth, notoriety, place, and power are no measures of success whatever. The only _true_ measure of success is the ratio between what we might have done or said on the one hand, and the things we did do and did say on the other hand."

(3) If when I get to heaven Jesus says,
    "Well done, thou good and faithful
    (not 'successful') servant,"
    then I will know I was a success!

   Success is doing God's work God's way.
As we learn to commit all to Him--our
jobs, our families, our youth groups, and
ourselves--we won't have to worry about
being a "success" or a "failure." We
won't have to worry about becoming workaholics. We won't have to worry about
burning out or managing time. We only
have to concern ourselves with doing what
God wants us to do, when He wants us to do
it. And we discover that each day contains
new challenges--and new rewards.

Time to Respond

1. How many hours do you work each week? Are you addicted to work?

2. If you have workaholic tendencies, how can you change your lifestyle?

3. Does your calendar contain regularly scheduled times of rest? If not, when are the best times for you to take off?

4. Does your supervisor understand your need for rest and relaxation? How can you make him more aware of your situation?

5. How can you increase the quantity and quality of time you spend with your children and/or your spouse?

6. When was the last time you had a good talk with your parents?

7. Discuss the "Diary of a Mad Housewife" article with your spouse. What steps can you take to prevent similar problems in your own marriage?

8. What is your measure of success?

9. How do you respond to failure?

10. During difficult times in your ministry, what are some positive events from the past that you can recall to carry you through the rough times?

FOCUS ON PEOPLE

CHAPTER FIVE

IF YOU'RE SO PEOPLE-ORIENTED, WHY DOES YOUR ONLY YOUTH GROUP MEMBER HAVE FOUR LEGS?

The ideas in this book have centered around providing practical ways for you to manage time and avoid burnout. But we all know that youth work is not built on timetables, programs, and organizations. It's built on relationships.

You will experience times in your youth ministry when all your plans go haywire because a young person needs you. That's OK. Goal-oriented youth workers must also be person-oriented, or they cannot be effective.

A letter written to a young Christian activist by Thomas Merton contained this excerpt: "You may have to face the fact that your work will be apparently worthless, and may even seem to achieve no results at all. . . . In the end it is the reality of personal relationships that saves everything. All the good that you will do will come from the fact that you have allowed yourself in obedience in faith to be used by God's love."

A few years ago, Faith at Work magazine featured the following article:

Then Came Susan

Grandmother's living room was large and dark. She kept the shades down so her
furniture wouldn't fade. One day in 1943, when I was five years old, I sat in
the middle of her living room floor playing with my toy cars. I had at least a
hundred: fire trucks, buses, tractors, everything--even a hearse.

For me playing cars was serious business. It took at least two hours at a
time. The idea was to form the largest possible circle of cars on the living room
floor. And the cars had to be evenly spaced. Precision was of the essence.

I placed my toy box in the middle of the floor. Then I took each car out of
the box--one by one. When all the cars were on the floor I began forming my
circle. I was very careful. No two fire trucks could be together. No two cars
the same color could be together. It was a tedious process but I was a determined
kid. When the circle was complete I sat in the middle and admired my cars and
my handiwork. And since Grandmother never used the living room, my circle
remained intact for days. I returned time and time again to look at my cars and
to make minor aesthetic adjustments--the red pick-up looks better behind the
dump truck . . . the jeep seems a little out of line, and so forth.

One morning I was sitting in the middle of my circle. Peace and content-
ment bathed my five-year-old soul as I surveyed my almost perfect toy kingdom.
Then came Susan. Susan was my three-year-old cousin. And she was a live wire.

Susan took one look at my circle of toys and charged. My precious, tranquil
circle was destroyed in an instant. She kicked and threw all my cars all over
the room. She was laughing and squealing--I was crying and screaming. Grandmother dashed in to see who was being murdered.

Grandmother later told me I cried for two hours. And she had to rock me
to sleep that night. How can you sleep when your world has been destroyed?

The next morning I went to the living room to survey the damage. My cars were
scattered all over the living room floor. I began the slow, painful process of
rebuilding. But when Grandmother told me Susan was coming over again, I gave up
in despair. So when my rambunctious little cousin arrived, there was nothing to
destroy. Susan suggested we take the cars outside. What an idea! I hadn't thought of
that. But what if they get dirty? What if one of my precious toys gets lost or
broken? It wasn't my idea of playing cars, but I gave in. I decided to risk
taking my cars outside. No use trying to build a circle with Susan around.

We played outside all day. We put real dirt in the dump truck. We shoved the
cars across the front porch as hard as we could. We made ramps, and forts, and
tunnels. I even let Susan talk me into crashing cars together. I had no idea
playing cars could be so much fun.

A lot of water has gone under the bridge since that day in 1943. I have
listened to hundreds of sermons and Sunday School lessons. I have read stacks
of theology books. A seminary degree hangs on my office wall. But I think
Susan taught me all I really know about theology--faith is the freedom to leave
the dark, musty living room and risk what you love most in the great outdoors.
(Wes Seelinger, Faith at Work, March 1974, p. 17. Used with permission.)

Every youth group should have a Susan, who takes the leader's nose out of paperwork, organizational meetings, reports, and agendas, and helps him to focus on what really matters--people!

The Apostle Paul's "Susan" was named Timothy. Paul described Timothy by saying, "I have no one else like him who takes a genuine interest in your welfare" (Philippians 2:20). Think of it. Of all the acquaintances the Apostle Paul had, there was no one on par with Timothy. Why? Because Timothy genuinely cared about people.

So even though the <u>contents</u> of this book have focused on impersonal topics like "time management" and "burnout," the <u>purpose</u> of the book is to help you spend more time with the <u>people</u> who matter to you. And if the time comes when you feel that black cloud of burnout creeping over your horizon, I hope the love for those young people you work with will sustain you. May their giggles and smiling faces (or their tears and broken hearts) bring fresh life to your soul and rekindle your purpose for being once more.

Time to Respond

1. Who are some of the "Susans" in your youth group or among your peers who take your nose out of paperwork?

2. How much time do you spend <u>in preparation</u> to meet with people? How much <u>time</u> do you <u>actually</u> spend with people?

3. Are you satisfied by the amount of time you spend with people? If not, look at your calendar to decide how you can schedule more "people time."

I DON'T KNOW WHAT'S WRONG. I JUST HAVE TROUBLE FORMING NORMAL RELATIONSHIPS.